1,033

REASONS TO

1,033
REASONS TO

ELIZABETH DUTTON

SKYHORSE PUBLISHING

Skyhorse Publishing books may be purchased in bulk at special
discounts for sales promotion, corporate gifts, fund-raising, or
educational purposes. Special editions can also be created to
specifications. For details, contact the Special Sales Department,
Skyhorse Publishing, 307 West 36th Street, 11th Floor, New York, NY
10018 or info@skyhorsepublishing.com.

Skyhorse® and Skyhorse Publishing® are registered trademarks of
Skyhorse Publishing, Inc.®, a Delaware corporation.

www.skyhorsepublishing.com

10 9 8 7 6 5 4 3 2 1

Library of Congress Cataloging-in-Publication Data is available on file.
ISBN: 978-1-61608-365-6

Printed in China

1,033

REASONS TO

The world, I am sure you will agree, is a
weird and wonderful place. There seems to
be collectively more good than bad in society,
otherwise we wouldn't all still be here. However,
there are times when the insanity or the anguish
or the confusion or the evil are just too much for
the everyman (and everywoman) to bear. When

this world and the other fragile humans that populate it overwhelm us, when life is painful or even simply boring, we need to be reminded of the weird and wonderful. The weird and wonderful are what make us smile, and those smiles keep us going. Smiles are pretty much universal—no matter your language or culture, a smile at its core means friendship, happiness, and ease. What follows are reasons to smile, simple as that. The title quantifies the reasons, but within these pages are far more and far fewer than 1,033 reasons to slap a grin on your gorgeous mug; everyone's smile mileage will vary. It is safe to say, though, that you'll find something in here to put a smile on your face. And if not? Then maybe you can smile with satisfaction at having been impervious to these attempts. Whatever gets you there, the object here is to smile.

★ Kittens in boxes. Even those who are allergic to cats have to admit that a small, fluffy kitten playing, sleeping, or just sitting in a box is pretty cute. Why the box? The cute is concentrated then, contained in one little cute space. And focused cute deserves a smile.

★ Finding money in a pocket. You know how this goes: you put on a coat you haven't worn in months, put your hand in the pocket and feel something there. This time, though, it's not an old tissue or a receipt. It's cash. Beautiful, forgotten cash.

★ Wrong number calls from super polite old ladies. You answer the phone. "Is Hegatha there?" As your name isn't Hegatha, you tell the caller, "No, I think you have the wrong number." Instead of a mumbled "oh" or just the click of the call disconnecting, the caller says in a frail, sweet, I'll-bake-you-some-cookies voice, "Well, my goodness. I am so sorry to bother you! Have a pleasant day." And you will, because now you are smiling.

Baby animals. Tiny, adorable, not yet deadly or painfully ugly.

 Baby animals wrestling. Tiny, adorable, tumbling around without a care in the world.

★ Baby animals shooting machine guns. Maybe a little scary, but sort of funny to imagine, right?

★ Getting back into your own bed after being away from home. Travel for pleasure is great, travel for business . . . not so much. But one thing they have in common is that when the trip has ended and you are no longer sleeping in a strange bed (which you've tried not to imagine the look of under a black light) or a friend's couch and you get to crawl back under your own covers, there is a certain bliss that (no matter how lumpy your own mattress may be) comes with knowing that you are home.

★ Dapper old men. Old men do dapper like no one else. Young guys just don't have the suave gravitas to pull it off. When an older gentleman dons a suit and hat to ride a train and graciously gives up his seat to a younger person (even though you know his bones ache and he'd rather be wearing sweats and fleece slippers), you can't help but smile at the way he keeps it real. Real cool.

★ Seeing the person in the car next to you singing along with their radio at the top of their lungs. Everybody has that song they love that they can't help but sing along to. And some people get so overwhelmed with the awesomeness flooding their ears that they forget about the outside world and just belt it out. That's a boundless, unrestrained happiness that for sure deserves a smile.

★ Inside jokes. We all have them with family or friends: a word or phrase that has a story too long to explain and is most likely one of those "you had to be there" moments, but that to this day can make you laugh.

★ When consumer advocate segments on the local news really skewer the bad guy and help the victim. There is such satisfaction in seeing the underdog win for once and seeing the evil, mustache-twirling bully get his or her comeuppance.

★ When you get in the car and your favorite song has just started on the radio. You LOVE this song. They never play it. It just started. Smile.

★ The look on Mike Myers' face when Kanye West said George W. Bush didn't care about black people. It was shock, it was confusion, it was fear, it was agreement. It was hilarious.

★ The Auto Correct feature on the iPad changes "Awwwwww" to "Asses." This is funny and makes you smile when you catch it before you send out the response to the picture of your friend's/ cousin's/neighbor's baby. And maybe it's still a little funny when you don't catch it before you hit "send."

★ Imagining Keith Richards at a parent/teacher
conference. We have all these rock stars who
live wild lives and have raucous images. They
also, though, usually have kids. Some aren't too
involved with their kids' lives, but a surprising
number are. Imagine Keith Richards at a parent/
teacher conference or a recital and you can't help
but smile at the dichotomy.

★ Holding the hand of someone you fancy for the
first time. Ah, this is electric bliss. And even the
memory of electric bliss merits a smile.

★ First kisses. More electric bliss.

★ Emails from long-lost friends. You see a name in your inbox that you haven't seen or thought about in ages. They've reached out across the years and made a connection and obviously you made an impact on them. That enduring link is one of the coolest things about humanity.

★ Sitting in first class. Everything is more comfortable and comfort makes you smile.

★ The smell of freshly cut grass. It smells clean (smile for clean), fresh (smile for fresh), and means things are growing and living (double smile for that).

★ Finding shapes in the clouds. We did this as kids—watched the clouds shift into discernable shapes, taking on the look of everyday or fantastic objects. It may seem a little cutesy and hipsterish to do now, but try it. It's even better when you have someone with you. It's still pretty cool and will still make you smile. Especially if you see something naughty.

★ Kids who hear live music and can't help but dance. You've seen this. You are at some farmers' market or festival and there's a stage on which some local band plays a cover song that most passersby let flow by them without notice. But then there's some kid, usually a toddler. The music is absolutely infectious to this child and he or she is unable to prevent knees from bending and arms from pumping. Total slave to the rhythm and it's awfully sweet.

★ Dogs in blankets. Dogs get cold, too, you know. And some dogs like being wrapped in a blanket. Swaddled puppy smile.

★ Old couples in love. For the jaded and world-weary who've had their hearts cast aside like some sort of non-biodegradable bag of chips, it is still a bit reassuring to see two elderly people who really, truly love each other no matter what. That love does exist and knowing that makes you smile.

Pre-teen boys getting nervous around pre-teen girls. They guffaw, they nudge each other, they strut, they preen. It's like an episode of *Wild Kingdom*. Except it's in a mall and the anxious sincerity of it all is enough to make anyone smile. At the very least, because we lived through it.

★ When kids mispronounce words or just make them up. There's just something irresistibly endearing about a kid very confidently announcing that her juice is "in the frijadader" or that he wants his "Buffer Baby book" (which after much confusion is translated as an alphabet book that contains the page "B for Baby").

★ Rainbows. Prismatic pot of gold and end of storm smile.

Double rainbows! Double smile! And maybe even a Youtube video.

 Watching a bumblebee struggle flying because of legs loaded down with pollen. C'mon, that's just precious.

★ When the person in the next lane lets you ahead of them in heavy traffic. That sort of unexpected kindness is sure to give you a smile. And then maybe you'll do the same for someone else and then *they* will smile and pretty soon Haley Joel Osment (whatever happened to him?) is there and we're all passing it on and smiling like fools and loving it. And maybe seeing dead people? I don't know.

★ When someone who looks tough or scary does something very gracious and kind. Tough looking guys with prison-style neck tattoos helping a stranger struggling to load something into his or her car. Smile at the unexpected.

★ Checking the calendar on a Friday and realizing that Monday is a holiday. Sweet relief.

Amazing sunsets. Whether you are watching the sky burn orange and red as the sun dips behind mountains or waiting for the mythical green flash at the moment the sun dips into the horizon on the Pacific Ocean, it's a gorgeous way to say goodbye to another day and hello to another evening.

Watching pigeons fight over a Cheeto. Kind of gross, but kind of funny.

★ Hearing that someone is newly cancer-free. This is a welcome change from expected bad news and a victory for that person and everyone who loves them. This for sure gets a smile or two.

★ Blooper reels over the credits at the end of a movie. Whether the movie was good or not, it is always kind of nice to see that everyone messes up on the job, no matter what they do. And they laugh about it, too.

★ Wildflowers. No one went out and planted them in that spot. No one tends to them or makes sure they're watered and fertilized. They just happen. Little wonders of color in sometimes unlikely places. Extra smile if it's a field of California poppies, which look like cups of molten gold and sunshine.

★ People who drive around with their cat in the car. They are making the bold move away from the typical dog with lips a-flapping in the wind out a car window. They are opting, instead, for a usually pudgy cat stretched out on the dashboard or pressed against the rear window. Either way, kudos to them for doing their own thing.

★ When kids get new shoes and are convinced they can now run faster. This is excitement over getting something new and all your own, but also that fantastically innocent mythical thinking that the impossible is not so.

The names of Popeye's four nephews are Pipeye, Peepeye, Pupeye, and Poopeye. Thank you, E. C. Segar (the creator of Popeye) for the chuckles.

 Just like fingerprints, everyone's tongue print is different. Yes, this has apparently already been on an episode of *CSI:NY*. But it's still pretty cool.

★ Legend has it that Babe Ruth wore a cabbage leaf under his baseball hat to keep him cool. I don't know if it's true or not, but it's weird enough to make me smile.

★ In the year 2000, Pope John Paul II was named an "Honorary Harlem Globetrotter." 50,000 people attended a ceremony in St. Peter's Square for the announcement of this honor. Another honorary Globetrotter? Henry Kissenger.

★ Realizing that Guy Fieri is the fifth Horseman of the Apocalypse. This realization will put a smile on your face because now you are able to pin down exactly what it is about him that is so revolting. He's a harbinger of the end times.

★ People who call soap operas "my stories." This is rather sweet, no?

★ Saffron-robed monks in urban settings. It's the juxtaposition of Buddhist serenity with frenetic city life that brings out the weird and wonderful and, therefore, the smiles.

★ The smell of the detergent aisle at the supermarket, where every fresh-scented perfume collides and manages to not smell like a French whorehouse.

★ Finding someone else's grocery list in your cart. It's a peek into someone else's life and priorities, a tender and harmless voyeurism.

★ Tiny dogs walking really fast. They mean business. They have to take five steps for every one step of their larger counterparts. Busy legs smile.

Finding the tipping point to solving a puzzle. Come on nerds, you know what I'm talking about. It's that one piece of the jigsaw that makes everything start to come together. It's the square in the Sudoku that makes everything fall into place. It's the 43 Across you thought was so impossible in that crossword but that now makes all the Down clues make sense. It's the sweet victory of all the gears in your brain turning at the right time in the right place.

Two words: open bar.

★ Going to an event and finding out that the free food there is actually really good. You have to go to this grand opening/retirement party/ promotional junket/random celebration. You figure you'll make your appearance, chat a bit, and then bypass the melon cubes/floppy shrimp/ cold meatballs and get a regular dinner. But what do you know? The food on hand is actually really good. And there are actually places to sit and interesting people to talk with. That totally rates a smile.

Baby/kid pictures that once really embarrassed you as a teenager. You can almost admire your overbite or your bare bottom in the bathtub or your inappropriately short shorts now, but the existence of these pictures signaled the end of life as you knew it when you were a teenager. You wanted them destroyed. Sure, your smile now may be a little bittersweet, but you can also smile because you didn't tear them to shreds and you eventually came to like your overbite and you wear clothes that fit now and no overzealous photo clerk reported your parents to the feds for kiddie porn. Whew.

★ Old men with obviously dyed hair. Give them credit (and a smile) for trying.

★ The sweet, plastic smell of the Sanrio store and the effect is has on little girls. For most six-year-old girls, the smell of the Sanrio store is like crack. They would huff the air in there, if they could. It's better than being excited by actual crack or inhalants, so that's good.

★ Cats who stare at you with distrust from windows or porches. I love the "STRANGER ALERT" look they give you, as if kidnapping an overweight, crusty-eyed tabby was at the top of your "to do" list for the day.

★ Green buds on trees at the start of spring. It's all possibility at this point, that starting place we all desire.

★ Finding an intact shell on the beach. Sure, the pieces you find are pretty. But the whole shell is remarkable. Smile for the beauty of it, smile because it made it through the surf, smile because you are holding a former home in your hands.

★ People who sing when they are drunk. Singing drunks are a million times better than angry or sullen drunks.

Kids who sing sea shanties. Sea shanties were songs sung by wizened sailors of yore, meant to keep time in the era when muscle alone kept ships moving and sails flapping in the wind was the only other sound you'd hear on the open ocean. The guys who sang them and made them up were tough, grizzled men and the lyrics ran from bawdy to godly. Today, sea shanties are seen as relatively tame and old-timey and lots of elementary school kids sing them as part of music education. There's something endearing about these soft souls singing the same lines and melodies as hardened workers who'd seen it all and then some.

★ Saying "cheese." Of course.

★ Saying "wee ah wee wee wee" also approximates a smile.

★ Making a wish from an eyelash. Blowing something so ephemeral and delicate from your fingertip out into the world with the hopes of something personal and secret attached is both sweet and hopeful. And worth a smile.

★ Reminding yourself that at least you aren't one of the *Real Housewives of Orange County*. Seriously, no matter how crappy your life is right now, take comfort in the fact that you aren't on that show. And if you are one of the cast members, have the person reading you these sentences skip to the next one.

★ When you have to pee really bad and you finally find a bathroom. Sweet relief if there ever was some.

★ When you finally find a public bathroom and it's way nicer and cleaner than you expected. This is even sweeter relief. We've all taken the "any port in a storm" stance and used a sketchy commode in an emergency. But when that emergency is resolved in a clean and even luxurious place? Jackpot.

Watching chickens run. It's a quick waddle and it's hilarious.

 Getting a raise. Smile because your economic life got a little easier, but also smile because you are getting your due recognition and maybe even for being the great person you are.

★ Remembering being a kid on long road trips and imagining you had a blade that would slice through trees and mountains and signs. Was that just me?

★ Road trip food. There are certain things you eat only when you are on the road, items you wouldn't think of buying on your regular trip to the grocery store. Slushy drinks. Beef jerky. Weirdly moist muffins wrapped in cellophane. All purchased in the flickering fluorescent light of a gas station. All tokens of that strange time spent getting from one place to another.

★ Carnival food. This is more food that you would never eat anywhere else. Corn dogs. Cotton candy. Funnel cake. All carnival food is horrible for you and all of it tastes great when you are eating it. It may make you feel like hell later, but for that moment when you are pulling a tuft of cotton candy from the paper cone and placing it on your tongue to dissolve, it's pure abandon.

★ Good luck charms. The little talisman brings you luck and comfort and a smile when you hold it in your hand.

★ Super large snowflakes. Falling snow warrants a smile, especially if it's the first of the season. But when the flakes of snow are unusually large, it's like a treat. A weird, frozen, floating treat.

★ Good hair days. No mystery cowlicks. No strangely flattened one side. No over or under use of product. Everything in its right place, even if it's supposed to look a mess. It's how you want it and as a result you feel great.

★ Carnie names like "Claw Hammer" and "Sugar Foot." If you are going to run away with the carnival and spend your pocket money on methamphetamines, energy drinks, and chewing tobacco, you might as well get yourself a fanciful, yet appropriately dirt-baggish name.

★ Eating fruit right from the tree or vine. Sometimes it's easy to forget that berries don't come into the world in plastic boxes or that apples don't grow with those little oval stickers on them. Getting fruit right from the source is a very simple pleasure that not enough of us get to enjoy.

★ People who buy sweaters for their cats. These wonderful weirdoes have gone beyond the realm of strange pet owner into a land all their own. They know the cat hates it, but they do it anyway. They are driven by an unknown force and I say we smile in honor of them letting their freak flag fly. And then we'll smile again, this time maybe wincing a little, when we hear about how their cat clawed their face to shreds at three in the morning.

Clean sheets on a freshly made bed. Comfort and calm. And no one's head sweat on the pillow cases.

 Getting a job done way ahead of the deadline. Stress averted deserves lots of smiles.

★ Hell's Angels blocking Westboro Baptist from protesting. When the Hell's Angels, who generally have no regard for social structure or morals, decide that you have crossed the line by waving offensive signs at the funerals of soldiers killed in action and bullied gay teens, you know you've messed up and messed up good. When you keep up that behavior and the biker gang has to come in and physically block you from causing more pain to grieving families, you pretty much get what you deserve.

★ "Thank you" cards. Not enough people send them. Not enough people receive them.

★ Free samples. Whether you are out running errands and someone hands you a free bag of trail mix in a store or you get a free pack of dryer sheets in the mail, it's nice to get something free once in a while.

★ No line at the DMV. This mythical occurrence actually does happen, usually at rural offices in the middle of the week. But still.

★ Oddly worded spam emails. "USA Dr. Amazing Is Your Dream Job Viagra." Smile. Delete.

★ Completing a crossword puzzle. That's some lovely satisfaction right there.

★ Completing a crossword puzzle in ink. That's some lovely, confident satisfaction right there.

★ Hearing a drink open in a movie theater. Someone's having a good time.

★ Getting a Wi-Fi signal when you thought there wouldn't be one. You don't expect to be able to pass the time playing Words With Friends or reading status updates. But there it is, the unsecured signal right there for the taking. Brilliant.

★ Seeing the weird things your neighbors call their Wi-Fi. "Police Van." "Cool Guy." "Stop Using My WiFi."

★ Bruises shaped like things. You got injured, so that's not really smile-worthy. But the result of banging your arm on your bike's handlebars is a bruise that looks like Pac Man. So there's the upside.

★ The underdog winning. Solidarity smile.

★ When your flight arrives significantly early due to "tail winds." One would think that the pilots and navigators would have all these variables figured out, but then there you are at the gate twenty minutes early. Don't complain or wonder why. Just smile.

★ Hearing someone quote a movie you love and no one else gets it. It's like a secret nod from one kindred spirit to another. Especially if the movie is *Waiting for Guffman*.

The mechanic tells you it was just a simple fix and the cost is low. Totally unexpected and a relief. So smile.

★ Watching babies eat something sour for the first time. No one can say that face isn't funny.

★ Weird notations in used books. Cryptic scribbles, talking back to characters, totally unrelated notes to themselves—this look into someone else's experience with a book is interesting and worth a smile.

★ When strangers help strangers. You can't help but smile at shared humanity. We're human, after all.

Priests who tell dirty jokes. Priests are humans, too.

The Jerky Boys. Smile because they elevated the crank call to new heights and smile because they are hilarious.

Birds in birdbaths. It is to be expected, but there's something very gentle about birds bathing. And in public! Oh, the scandal.

 Kids crayon scribbles in books. The Julia Child recipe for Beef Bourguignon is covered in waxy yellows and greens. They wanted to contribute, they really did.

★ Pets with boring people names. Cats named Larry, dogs named Susan—these beat Fluffy and Spot any day.

★ Hearing someone fart in church. Church is often a solemn affair filled with human beings who do human things. I think God would have a sense of humor about someone ripping one in church. I mean, anyone who created the honey badger likes a good laugh.

★ Cotton candy. It's pure sugar, so it's not in any way good for you. But that odd chemistry of sugar crystals made into a puffy cotton that melts away on your tongue is worth a smile.

★ Putting on warm clothes right from the dryer on a cold morning. To go from the rigid irritation of no longer sleeping and feeling chilled to the syrupy comfort of toasty clothes is rather heavenly.

★ Butterflies. You can smile because of the colors or because of their transformation origin or because of the drunken way they flit through the air. Butterflies, while often the inspiration for bad tattoos, are a pretty much endless resource for smiles.

★ The flashing light on the Capitol Records building in Los Angeles spells HOLLYWOOD in Morse Code. Sheer uselessness yet pure Southern California flash.

★ The feel of cashmere. Light and luxurious and about as soft as it gets. Smile.

★ Hearing about a very messy murder scene. This one only applies to psychopaths and crime scene cleanup companies.

★ Grown men painting their faces for a professional sporting event. There's something very sincere about the excitement and dedication it takes to actually slap your favorite team's colors on your face and scream your head off for them to win. Extra points if they make it on television with their display and are seen by friends and family (or, sadly, co-workers).

★ Remembering the ridiculousness of Ben Affleck in the JLo years. Seriously, how hilarious was he as an over-groomed, track-suited mouth breather? His funniest role in years.

★ Old school hip hop. Rap and hip hop have come a long way from the basic beats of yesteryear. Those stilted, elemental rhymes changed music and popular culture.

★ Digital watches. Still cool. Still worth a smile.

Celebrity schadenfreude. It's great to see a famous person get their comeuppance.

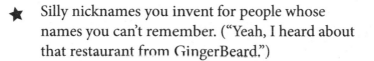 Silly nicknames you invent for people whose names you can't remember. ("Yeah, I heard about that restaurant from GingerBeard.")

Dogs chasing Frisbees. Smile for the dog getting super excited, smile for when the dog jumps to catch it and misses.

Imagining cows walking around on their hind legs. Kind of freaky, kind of funny.

★ Fourth grade science projects. The best projects are the ones that have no obvious parental tampering. Poster board triptychs with glitter and hand-lettered titles. Colored pencil graphs and pasted photocopied photos. Job well done, little scientists.

★ Watching movies outside on a summer night. There's really nothing like watching an old film projected on a wall under the stars while mockingbirds sing and crickets chirp away. Lots of extra smiles if fireflies show up.

Kids in parades. It's a big deal for them and their smiles show it.

 Shriners in parades. Tiny cars and fezzes? Sign me up.

 Trannies in parades. Trannies bring the fun.

★ Tranny Shriners in parades. If only.

★ Local festivals. Small towns should be able to celebrate just being a small town. However, they always seem to have something else to be proud of and want to honor with a party: watermelons, bales of hay, unique geographical location, almonds, you name it. Festivals are a great excuse to walk around in the sun and smile.

★ Blimps. Such an unlikely mode of transportation. When you see a blimp overhead, though, you know that there's some sort of major entertainment afoot somewhere nearby and even the most jaded will look up in awe at the weird, giant balloon in the sky.

★ Fireworks finales. Let 'er rip, boys!

★ Soccer/football announcers freaking
out over a goal. It can be a small match
between two insignificant teams or it can
be a battle over the UEFA cup. Either way,
GOOOOOOAAAAAAAAAALLLLLLLLL!!!!!!!

★ Big tips (if you are a waiter/waitress). It's nice to
be appreciated.

★ The seat next to you staying empty on a plane. Extra room. And for free. Smile.

★ When you think someone is calling to complain, but they are actually calling to thank or compliment you. This unexpected turn of events is enough to make your day, sometimes. Avoiding a problem and hearing something nice? Smile city.

★ Driving a convertible with the top down on a nice day. It's not the time to worry about your hair. Just smile and thank whoever it was that invented the convertible.

★ Having a favorite pen. This is a nerdy reason to smile, but a reason nonetheless. Everyone has specific preferences when it comes to writing utensils and most people have that one pen that they love, that fits nicely in their hand, and somehow makes your handwriting look even better. It's nice to have a favorite something.

Going to buy something you need and finding out there's a big sale. You need trash bags. And is it just me or have garbage bags gotten kind of pricey? The moment you use them, they are garbage themselves. Whatever. You head to the store to get some and what do you know, they are 60 percent off. Score. Smile.

★ Finding a really cool pair of shoes and the last available pair is in your size and on sale. Bingo.

Goofy local weathermen. They provide the one piece of news that impacts everyone and they still dress it up with goofy slogans and strange ads. Bonus smile if the weatherman goes into full weather geek mode because of unusual weather in the area.

 Diagonal crosswalks. This is when all auto traffic has to stop and the pedestrian free-for-all begins. Head whichever way you want on foot, the intersection is yours.

★ Standing in the sun on a cold day. Extra smile if you are wearing something dark that soaks up the heat.

★ Waking up naturally before your alarm goes off. Your body has bested technology and you are ready for the day. No rude awakenings for you, just smiles.

★ Short guys who wear heeled boots. There's something endearing about height-impaired men who want that extra lift, so they don boots with heels. They aren't fooling anyone, nor are they trying to. Cute.

★ Kids singing along with Bob Dylan songs. This doesn't happen enough.

★ Popping bubble wrap. Mindless smiles.

★ When you realize your headache has gone away. This realization of sweet relief is worth a smile or two.

★ Seeing someone blow a really big chewing gum bubble. And an extra smile if it pops and spreads a sheen of bubble gum across the face. And an extra extra smile if the gum doesn't get stuck in their hair.

★ Finding a parking space right in front of your destination, especially in a big city. This is a blessing, a karmic gift, an alignment of the universe. There are at least a thousand smiles in this event alone. Jackpot.

Cannonball Run, Scavenger Hunt, and other 1980s ensemble zany comedies. Corny dialogue, ridiculous plots, mindless fun.

 Cracking the sugar on top of a crème brûlée.

★ Kids getting excited about pushing elevator buttons. As adults, elevators are just a means to an end, a time to look at your shoes and avoid eye contact with that weird guy in the corner. But kids see it as an opportunity to pilot the ship and get drunk with the power to decide where this large machine stops. Extra smiles if everyone lets them have their fun with it.

★ Pain medication. Pain is lame. Floating away from pain on a pharmaceutical cloud is smile town.

★ Seeing rolling papers in the kitchen drawer at your grandmother's house. Granny's a toker. Good for her.

★ Foot massage chairs at county fairs. It's just a chair with a jiggling metal plate on which to rest your weary feet after hours of strolling around on blacktop. But that foot vibration feels damn good amidst the calls of guys selling magic vegetable choppers and screams coming from riders on roller coasters assembled by a crack team of possible crackheads.

★ Cats don't have opposable thumbs. Whew. We dodged a bullet on that one.

★ Novelty car horns. Not only does the owner like the tune so much they made it their car horn, they paid actual money to have it installed. There is no question, though, that hearing one is pretty funny.

★ A really great latte. The espresso is perfectly brewed, the milk is expertly steamed, there's just the right amount of foam and the temperature is just how you like it. Little pleasures.

★ Catching something that is falling before it hits the ground. A nice save deserves a nice smile.

★ Tossing something into the garbage can and making it. You may have been picked last for every sport in elementary school or maybe you rode the bench all season for your high school ·basketball team, but landing that apple core into the bin makes you feel like a superstar.

★ Little kids with foreign accents. So tiny, and yet so worldly.

★ Random stuff woven into a bird's nest. Clipped hair from the sidewalk in front of the barber shop, strips of old plastic tarps, thread, shoelaces . . . birds will make anything work. And remember, they do this all with just their beaks and little feet. Amazing.

★ Tattooed death metal enthusiasts who quote *The Princess Bride*. Seriously, there's nothing cuter than a guy in a Sabbath t-shirt saying "You keep using that word. I do not think it means what you think it means," when you say "inconceivable." As you wish . . .

★ Finding out the person interviewing you for a job went to the same high school or college as you did. Oh, fates, you are too kind sometimes.

★ Free upgrades. Here, have a better room at this hotel. Have a better rental car. Let's move you up to first class. Oh, no charge. Smile.

★ Come-from-behind wins on *Jeopardy*. Basically, any underdog victory deserves a smile, especially one in the presence of the world's most (only?) obnoxious Canadian, Alex Trebek.

★ Imagining Tom Cruise and Iggy Pop power walking together around a track. It's a weird image.

★ Imagining the Queen of England falling down drunk. I could see this. There's no telling what kind of hooch she's got stashed in her pocketbook.

★ Imagining Gwenyth Paltrow breakdancing for spare change on a sidewalk. Of course, it would be on the *finest* sustainable cardboard, but still hilarious.

Seeing someone actually slip on a banana peel. Just like in the cartoons, but in real life. No smiles if they hurt themselves, though.

 Hearing a loud bang and realizing it was a car backfiring and not gunfire. That gets a smile of relief.

★ Flirty babies. Some people have been working the room since they were in diapers. They know how to get the attention and charm the pants off of anyone. Granted, their own pants are filled with their own filth, but that never stopped a real flirt.

★ Finding a forgotten beer or soda in the back of the refrigerator. You thought you were out. Think again. Smile.

★ Scoring super high on a Scrabble turn. Eighty points for one word? Big grin for your cleverness, bigger grin as your opponents grumble.

★ Getting a great haircut. We can all easily remember the bad haircuts we've had, the ones that took a little too much off the top or for some reason made our faces look lopsided. Let's pay tribute to the ones when you walk out of the salon and catch your reflection in the mirror and think, "Hot damn, I look good." Extra smiles if it happens the next day when you have to style the thing by yourself.

★ The sound of a bottle of champagne being opened. Party smile.

★ Fixing a computer problem all by yourself. Self-sufficiency smile.

★ Five-day weather forecasts where every day is mild and sunny. Smooth sailing smile.

★ Old photo albums. Sometimes the smiles from perusing an old photo album are bittersweet. Sometimes they are due to long-forgotten happy memories resurfacing. Sometimes it's just that reminder of how small you once were or how much you now look so much like a grandparent in their youth. Enjoy them all.

★ Other people's bad passport photos. There are some doozies and there's always someone with a passport photo worse than yours.

★ You aren't Lindsay Lohan. That's a relief.

★ No matter what you do, you are probably not as bad as Hitler. Smile! You aren't as terrible as a murderous dictator!

★ There's someone out there with the job title "fluffer." They may work in a pillow factory or they may work on a porno set.

★ Good dreams that stick with you all day. These sweet remnants of the otherworldly ramblings of your subconscious cling to you throughout the day like a loose piece of thread and make for pleasant distractions.

★ Someone thinks you are hot, even if it's your creepy old neighbor or that weirdo at the supermarket.

★ You only have to go through puberty once. That's a major relief.

★ Much like herpes, smiling is contagious. Someone smiles at you, you smile and then smile at someone else, they smile, and on and on. Pretty soon we're all grinning. And, unlike herpes, there are no sores involved.

Smiling reduces your blood pressure. This is SCIENCE. And science is pretty cool. So is lowering your blood pressure.

Even the worst day has to end some time. Plus, you'll look back and it won't seem so bad. I promise.

People-watching in the park. Seeing how other people go about their business, how they interact, what they wear and the things they say—all of this is a nice portrait of humanity. And humanity is deserving of lots of smiles.

You aren't the only one who forgets things. We all mess up.

In China, *Boogie Nights* translated to "His Powerful Device Makes Him Famous." Well, at least that's what it says on the Internet. Who knows if this is true. But it's funny if it is.

 Taking the moral high road and winning.

★ Fresh guacamole (if you like guacamole). This is heavenly if you are into it. If the thought of avocados makes you feel barfy, just skip to the next one.

★ Tech developments that make things really easy. Getting an answer to almost every question instantly, being able to talk to someone anywhere in the world (video) face to (video) face, quick messages, instant news. Life is a lot easier thanks to technology. Smile if you love technology. And for you Luddites, smile anyway.

★ Care packages. Someone sent you a box of the stuff that you like because, as it says in the name, they care. That's pretty nice and should get a smile.

★ Hand-written family recipes. Your grandmother's handwriting is fragile and precise and conveys the dish that no Thanksgiving would ever be without. Hold on to that.

★ Sunshine. Gives us the Vitamin D we need to make the calcium do its job. Lightens your mood. Highlights your hair. Not bad, right?

★ Finishing reading a really great novel. The story was compelling and the characters almost seemed real. What's even better is that some other human being thought all of that up and was able to convey it to you in words, communicating to you a vision that will now stay with you and make you think. That's just magic.

★ Seeing an ex who looks terrible. Part of the bitterness in a breakup is imagining your now ex running around, free as a bird and happy as a clam, and some other descriptive simile comparing them to a small living thing. Then you see them and they look like hell. And there's a part of you that thinks, "well, serves you right."

★ Imagining dogs being able to talk. Weird, maybe a little scary, but most likely quite humorous.

People who write with fountain pens. That's some elegant stuff right there.

 New notebooks. Empty pages are all possibility.

 People who write letters on typewriters. Fading fast, but clinging to a time gone by. Good on 'em.

People who repeatedly walk through the camera frame of live feeds on the local news. Yes, we see you. Yes, it's kind of funny.

 Getting BINGO. Chance in action.

★ Cupcakes. They are tiny cakes made just for one person. And tiny is usually cute. So we've got tiny, personalized, cute, sweet . . . lots of smiles in there.

★ Taking a boat being a necessary part of getting somewhere. This is a rare occurrence and one that should be savored and smiled upon.

Really old men with an ear pierced. What's up, cool dude?

 Old sailor tattoos. Not new versions on someone who has only seen the ocean from a beach chair. Blurred, greening tattoos on the forearms of old sailors. The real deal.

★ When the government does the right thing. We don't expect it and it certainly is nice to be pleasantly surprised.

★ Peaceful protests. Getting a message across without broken windows or bones is worth a smile.

Lounging clothes. These are not your pajamas. These are your comfortable clothes for when you know you won't have to leave the house and can just lounge around. Thus the name.

 People who swan about in caftans. Drama smile.

★ Laughing Indian babas. Holy men who live in the poorest conditions but have the happiest daily existences. They especially savor the absurd in everyday life, a good approach to take and one that can generate endless smiles.

★ Russian onion dome buildings. This is actually a marriage of form and function. Onion dome construction looks cool and can symbolize a candle, but it also keeps snow from piling up on the roof.

★ World Cup fever (minus the *vuvuzela*).

★ Someone telling a really sincere story for no reason. Some people may find this irritating. But look at it this way: the storyteller has some reason for wanting to spill his or her guts. And they aren't telling the tale to brag or embellish. So sit back and listen and smile that someone feels you are the right person, the one who will listen.

★ Jump rope songs. They can be innocent or even a little filthy, but the songs that keep the beat when jumping rope are sweet reminders of childhood and the omnipresence of music.

★ Chalk art on the sidewalk. Sometimes it's kids scribbling, sometimes it's talented artists rendering rich imagery. But it is impermanent and solely for the instant enjoyment of passersby. Smile.

★ Bad caricatures by street artists. You sit patiently while the artist sketches your image in charcoal. Tourists stroll by, glance at the work in progress, and continue on. You expect to have your nose or ears exaggerated, that's what comes with the territory. When you finally see the piece it looks NOTHING like you. You can smile because you've been had or you can smile because it's absurd or you can smile because the artist did they best they could.

★ *Star Wars* fanatics arguing over small details. They've seen the original three countless times. They've seen all six in order. They've read the books. They've mastered the video games. They own the card games. At least one of them is wearing a "Max Rebo Band" t-shirt. And they are arguing over whether the SFX guys on Empire used a potato or a painted beet as an asteroid.

★ Klonopin. Ah, smile.

Free refills. Want some more soda? Go ahead.

 Noticing that gas prices went down. Rare enough occurrence. Smile.

★ Unexpected package delivery. You didn't order anything recently. Must be a gift. Smile. Extra smile knowing it can't be from the Unabomber because he's in jail.

★ The mean things your friends say about your ex to make you smile. "Well, he *was* a wimpy asthmatic who totally didn't deserve you . . . "

Community gardens. People coming together to make something beautiful and useful in a disused place. Smile.

 That Ice-T went from singing "Copkiller" to playing a cop on *Law & Order: SVU*.

★ Fingerless lace gloves. Perhaps the least utilitarian piece of clothing ever. Absurd smile.

★ Crazy golf pants. Now that golf is a real sport, with athletic company sponsors and all that, the notion of guys wearing loud pants and playing through with the main goal of making it to the "19th Hole" for a martini or three is antiquated but sweet.

Silly names brothers and sisters have for each other.

 Your first instinct is almost always correct. This is true and a reason, for sure, to smile.

★ Getting your braces off. Ah, dental liberation!

★ Everyone thinks *Family Circus* is horrible. Everyone. So smile because sometimes nothing makes sense.

★ Cheap local business television ads, especially those with jingles. Remember, someone had to go into the studio and record the jingle. They had to sing about deals at the local Ford dealership . . . with FEELING. There's something very sweet about that.

Drinking lemonade on a porch in the South. This is very calming and certainly a reason to smile.

 Sitting on the beach in Malibu. This is as California as it gets and is a reason to smile.

 Eating lobster in Maine. Total cliché, but you are getting it from the source, so smile.

Buying a baguette in Paris. Extra smile if they are stereotypically rude to you.

 Eating pizza in Italy. So much better than Round Table.

 Drinking a Guinness in Dublin. It's not any fresher than that.

★ Drinking a lot of Guinness in Dublin.

★ Doting new fathers. They are overwhelmed and excited and involved. Lots of smiles for them.

★ Parents meeting their kids at the school bus. All-American smile.

★ Your name is Radical Coolguy. This only applies if your name really is Radical Coolguy. But you can also smile at the thought of someone adopting that as their name.

★ You could change your name to Radical Coolguy if you wanted to. You can take whatever name fits your fancy, as long as you go through the legal paperwork. That's pretty cool.

★ The early '90s double sock craze. Was this a trick on the part of the sock industry to move more product? Who knows, but it was absurd and smile-worthy.

★ Being nervous about a test and then sitting down to take it and finding it super easy. Piece of cake smile.

★ Amazing sunsets. Ending the day with splashes of orange, purple, and red across the sky is pretty amazing.

★ Amazing sunrises. If you are awake when the sun comes up, you either got up early or never went to sleep. Either one deserves a reward and the sun pushing up from the east to start the day is an awfully great one.

★ Tacky souvenirs. Do you need the bamboo back scratcher with "Kauai" painted on the handle? How about the framed hologram of a unicorn and dolphin mid-frolic your friend picked up for you at some tourist trap in Florida? And the keychain with a big plastic London taxi dangling from it? Tacky, but full of silly memories or reminders that someone thought about you as they traveled.

★ Thinking back to when you first heard about email. It didn't make sense, right? There were all sorts of steps you had to perform in order to retrieve the message. Why not just send a letter? Or call me? Ah, olden days.

★ Remembering your first cell phone. For some it was the big beige one the size of your face. For others it was the one kept in the car due to its toaster-sized battery pack. Fat flip phones, no color screens, roaming charges. But, man, was it exciting.

Pre-teen fashion risks. If you feel like wearing a tutu over your jeans or tying bandanas around your ankles, go for it.

★ Valentine candy hearts with misprints. It's supposed to say HOT STUFF but the T didn't print. Give it to the one you love.

Bizarre fortunes in fortune cookies. Every now and then you run across a little paper fortune that isn't so uplifting or positive. While others at the table get "You have an artistic mind and creative soul" or "Exciting travel awaits you," yours informs you, "The road to hell is paved with good intentions." In bed?

★ Lazy susans. Lazy utilitarian smile.

★ Super Bowl commercials. We marvel at how much it costs for thirty seconds of air time. We pick them apart, decide on our favorites. They are a weird entertainment within entertainment.

★ A paid day off. Do whatever you want and still get paid. Lots of smiles.

★ Outsider art. You have to smile for people who make art that is meaningful to them, even if it goes against everything the art school set has decided makes for "good art." Intent trumps skill and the artist makes it just for the hell of it.

★ Crafts. Smile for both the process and the end result. Sure, you could go out and buy that candle/mosaic/toaster cozy in some store, but there's sweetness to something made by hand.

Surfers. They live to ride a surge of ocean water. It's everything to them and that's rather endearing.

 Brunch. If you are eating brunch, you aren't in a hurry. Smile.

★ Taking the training wheels off. Balance achieved, along with big boy/girl status.

★ When people correct grammar mistakes on signs (guerrilla editing). Go ahead and add or remove that apostrophe. You are performing a public service.

★ Old hardware stores with wooden floors. You know the place has been there for some time. They carry things you didn't even know were made anymore. You also know that the old guys behind the counter know exactly what you'll need for whatever it is you are trying to fix or build and are happy to talk you through the process.

★ Being all warm and bundled up outside and seeing your breath.

★ Getting to work and seeing that someone brought doughnuts for everyone. You may not like doughnuts or maybe are trying to stay away from such carbohydrate bombs. But someone went out of their way on their trip to work to try and make a day at the office a little more bearable. Kind gestures always deserve smiles.

★ Tissue with lotion in it when you have a cold. No longer do you suffer the double indignity of being so stuffed up you can't pronoun words with the letter *n* in them and also having nostrils rubbed raw and angry.

★ Hearing someone explain a touchy subject to a kid. It's a high wire act, trying to explain death or sex or drunks to a kid without scarring them for life.

★ Your neighbor taking your trash can out for you, shoveling the snow from your driveway, or helping in some way just to be nice. Don't be suspicious. They don't want anything other than for you to smile.

★ Getting a paper invitation in the mail instead of an email or e-vite. Extra mile smile.

★ Eating something messy and not getting anything on your shirt. This can be quite a feat. Congratulations.

★ When a car alarm finally stops. You'd started wondering if you would ever know life without the shrill trilling of the neighbor's car alarm. There was no attempted theft, just the rumble of a passing muscle car to set off the sensitive system installed to protect the 1987 Accord with one headlight. Just when you think you can no longer stand it, blessed silence. Whew. Smile.

★ Someone you like putting their arm around you. Comfort smile.

★ Seeing-eye dogs. It's not just a cuddly companion, it's a cuddly companion that keeps its owner from getting hit by cars or tripping over steps.

★ The notion of a seeing-eye cat. All hell would break loose, or those without sight would never leave their windowsills. Still funny to imagine.

★ The heartbursting joy and relief expressed in Allen Ginsberg's "Footnote To Howl." Look it up and revel in it.

★ The sound of a train in the distance at night. People are traveling or goods are being moved on the rails as you drift off to sleep. There's an odd, happy melancholy to the sound of the train whistle in the darkness, heading off to who-knows-where.

★ Very tiny things. Tiny carrots, tiny horses, tiny doll house furniture . . . things in miniature are fascinating.

★ Unusually large things. Whether it's an 800-pound pumpkin or a six-foot-long pencil, things created or bred for no reason other than to see how large you can make something speak to some inner working of the human brain that wants to know what's on the outer edges of possible and ridiculous. Smile for that.

★ When friends see you from their cars as you walk down the street and they honk or catcall you. Smile because someone is excited to see you. Smile because it's not coming from strangers on a prison bus.

★ A fire in the fireplace on a cold night. Cozy smile.

★ Catching a whiff of someone's perfume that reminds you of someone you love. You are standing in the bread aisle of the supermarket when a lady walks by and in her wake leaves the trace of the exact perfume your grandmother always wore. You haven't smelled it in years but are immediately transported back to your childhood, remembering the signature scent of your parent's parent. Thanks for the memory and smile, anonymous lady in the supermarket.

★ Indoor plumbing. Let's take a moment and smile at the fact that we have running water indoors and don't have to go to an outhouse to relieve ourselves.

★ Watching a woodpecker at work. You hear a tapping and look up to see the bright red head of a woodpecker jackhammering away at a tree trunk. You can only hope the little headbanger is successful in his search for bugs.

Pets confused by a DVD tray opening and closing via remote. Teasing smile.

 Your pub trivia night team winning because one of you knew how to correctly spell the last name of Duke basketball coach Mike Krzyzewski. Obscure knowledge smile.

The perfect piece of chocolate cake. Flawlessness smile.

 Very tiny acorns. Something the size of a blueberry will grow into a thirty-foot-high oak tree. Nature is basically amazing.

★ Crazily detailed nail art. Those airbrushed sunsets or perfectly stylized daisies took a lot of time and make the wearer pretty happy. Give 'em a smile.

★ It has been recently determined that the computing power of all the general purpose computers in the world is the same as one human brain. Humans for the win.

★ Postcards. This means that someone thought of you while away, and that someone also happened to have your mailing address with them. And that someone took the time to get a stamp and mail their hello to you. Wish you were here smile.

★ They say that measured pound for pound, a baby is stronger than an ox. Super baby smile.

★ Legend has it there's a basketball court at the top of the Matterhorn ride at Disneyland. Does anyone ever play there? If so, who? Smile for the idea of someone shooting hoops while people speed by and scream on the ride. Smile for someone building something nonessential but fun into that big fake mountain in a place dedicated to the nonessential but fun.

★ Since it is impossible to lick your elbow, no one can stand next to you on the subway and lick their elbow.

★ The tune used for the National Anthem ("Star Spangled Banner") was originally an English drinking song. Which is why it's a great way to start sporting events.

★ George Orwell, author of *1984* and *Animal Farm* and a bit of a nutter, had random blue spots tattooed on the knuckles of one of his hands. Thomas Edison had five dots tattooed on his arm, arranged like you'd find them on the face of a die. He didn't want to explain what it meant, so no one knows. It's rumored that Winston Churchill's mom had a snake tattooed on her wrist. So if you have some ink that only makes sense to you or that maybe you regret a little, smile. You aren't alone.

When you are running errands, imagine you are in a montage scene from a bad '80s movie. Ridiculous mental image smile.

Putting on your favorite t-shirt. Whatever the reason for it ranking tops in your collection of tops, donning it certainly gets a smile.

People voluntarily cleaning up beaches or creeks. Community smile. And garbage-free critter zone smile.

 Ladies who wear fresh flowers in their hair. Added touch smile.

Electricity. We take this for granted, being able to turn on the lights, keep the refrigerator running, powering up our computers, etc. It's an expected luxury that needs some smiles in appreciation. Extra smiles for the utility workers who go out in the ice and tempests to turn that electricity back on when nature interrupts it.

 Boys with dolls. Progressive parent smile.

★ When oncoming traffic pulls over for an approaching funeral procession. This show of understanding and humanity reminds us that we're all connected.

★ Finding really strange books in used bookstores. *Sausage Making for the Whole Family* or *Corn Dogs and Caviar: My Life Story* may have had very limited print runs and were probably only initially purchased by relatives of the author, but for 50¢ it can be yours and is guaranteed to make your bookcase a whole lot more interesting.

★ You aren't in jail right now. And if you are, you are at least in a facility where you are allowed to read books about smiling, which is maybe not so bad . . . although I would recommend either fashioning a shiv out of the spine of this book or just putting it away where no one can see it, since it may attract unwanted attention in prison.

★ You don't have a sex tape that has leaked onto the Internet. Or, if you do, it's probably making some money so you've got that to smile about.

★ No one is currently shooting a gun at you, which is nice. If they are, it's probably a good idea to put the book down and take cover.

★ You are not currently in a burning building, which is also nice. Of course, if you are, you've got to get the hell out of there! Now! Stop, drop, and roll, too!

★ Seeing the sun reflect off little waves on the ocean is very calming and smile-inducing.

★ You didn't get trampled to death at a Target store last Black Friday. You've got that going for you.

★ Your life allows you time to read a book providing a large number of reasons to smile. If that's not leisure, I don't know what is.

★ You didn't have to come up with more than a thousand reasons to smile all by yourself, so in that way you are sort of like a benevolent potentate who receives appeasement of your every whim. And I live to serve, obviously.

You are not currently on stage at a poetry slam. That's a relief. For you and for the rest of us.

 Nor are you in the audience.

 You are not currently being murdered by a serial killer. (But, um, if you are and this book is part of his sick ritual, I am really, really sorry.)

★ Seeing teenagers all dolled up in cheap formal wear out for dinner before prom. It's a big night out full of satin and hair spray and aftershave and concealer and corsages and awkward meals and even more awkward attempts to walk in heels. Rite of passage smile.

★ When people laugh at your jokes. It feels good, right? You gave them a smile, so give yourself a smile.

Outdoor dining. Taking a meal in the fresh air and sunshine slows you down and relaxes you, something we all need. It also makes you smile, something we all really need.

 Hearing someone refer to someone else as a "cool customer." Any sort of antiquated phrase is unexpected and charming these days. Smile.

★ If you are standing in line at the DMV, you can smile because at least you don't work there and have to be there all day, every day. If you work at the DMV, you can smile because at least you get to go home at the end of the day. (They do let you go home at the end of the day, right?)

★ People are good. Sure, there is the minute percentage of people who exhibit violent madness or pure evil (see: Geoffrey Dahmer, Adolf Hitler, oil company executives) but for the most part, people are kind and good. After all, we celebrate kindness and goodness. There were no "feel good" stories about Michael Vick's interaction with animals.

★ The smell of steaks on a BBQ. Even vegetarians have to admit that smells good.

Birds singing in the morning. Going to be a good day smile.

Songbirds imitating frogs. Cute, right? Mockingbirds do this, particularly unmated males. They do this in the middle of the night, generally right outside my bedroom window. Especially when I have to wake up early. All they want, though, is a mate. And if it means stealing the song of another species, so be it. Good luck, young mockingbird dude.

★ Foggy mornings. The fog hovers above the ground almost like a blanket, as if the rest of the world around you didn't want to get out of bed, either. Solidarity smile.

★ Van de Graaf generators. These are those silver orbs that generate static electricity and when you put your hands on it, your hair stands on end. Good, clean, scientific fun smile.

★ Surprisingly frank alumni updates. These are rare, and their honesty is worth a few smiles. Instead of crowing about marriages, babies, promotions, or awards, these updates tell us that your former classmate lives in a decommissioned missile silo in Wyoming and composes operas on a theremin.

★ Reading funny names in the paper. The recipient of the Rotary Club award was Hank Corntower. And now you have a new alias, so there's that to smile about, too.

When people provide obviously fake names when interviewed for a local news story. "I think the new law is a good idea," said local resident Amanda Huggankiss.

 The excitement kids have on Christmas eve. Overwhelming anticipation smile.

The color yellow. It's supposed to be the happiest color. Lemons, bananas, sunshine, um . . . pee. Whatever. When you see it, smile.

 When Martha Stewart gets an attitude with her guests on the show. There's a reason it's called the *Martha Stewart Show*. It's all about Martha and woe unto the guest who annoys her.

★ Remembering that Martha Stewart has done hard time.

★ Imagining Martha Stewart pumping iron in a prison rec yard. She would, of course, fashion the weight bench from an old barn door and paint it robin's egg blue.

★ When people try hard not to fall asleep, but they can't help it and their heads nod forward violently. I know how you feel smile.

★ Almost 30 percent of Americans do some sort of volunteer work. It may not seem like a big percentage, but remember that everyone thinks we're lazy and probably expects 0 percent. Smile for helping others and smile for low expectations.

★ Some birds can see into the UV spectrum, seeing colors we can't. Wondering what we're missing smile.

★ Learning a new word. Your vocabulary is one word richer and you also love the way it sounds. Smile.

★ Going to the movies in the middle of the week in the afternoon. The place is empty. No one is elbowing you. No cell phones are going off. No one is eating nachos right behind you. Just you and the movie.

★ Imagining what life would be like if animals could talk. Noisy, for sure, but enlightening.

★ People with kind faces. These aren't always pretty faces, but some people just have a kindness about them, an openness, that is conveyed to everyone they meet. That's a great quality to have, one that induces a lot of smiles.

★ When dealing with a customer service rep on the phone, asking where they are and then discussing the weather in your different locations. It's a real person. Smile.

People with VERY specialized interests. Not just old movies, but pre-code gangster films. Not just flowers, but dwarf dahlias. Specificity smile.

Trees blooming in spring. New start smile.

★ Sand castles. Truly temporary construction performed during a time of leisure. Sometimes they are intricate, sometimes they are more of the mound variety. Either way, they are someone's vision of a castle. Extra smile if found items like shells or sea glass are used for accents.

★ Taco Tuesdays. Actually, we can also include Aloha Fridays here, as well. Designating a day of the week to something enjoyable (delicious food, loud shirts) is a simple, but smile-worthy, pleasure.

★ Men who wear novelty socks with formal suits. They feel a little wacky and they want you to know it. Let's celebrate their wackiness with a smile.

★ Remembering your favorite place as a child. We all have a place that we loved when we were little. Maybe a vacation spot, maybe a place on the sofa in the den. This location holds special, fond memories for you. You can remember how is smells and how everything felt. Hold on to that spot.

★ Remembering the late '80s/early '90s obsession with making things clear: phones, Pepsi, those plastic ties with sand and shells and blue gel in them that looked like the beach. At the time, it felt very futuristic and innovative. Hindsight smile.

★ Powerful people who don't take themselves seriously. Power corrupts, they say. But it also can make people into totally self-absorbed jerks. Here's a smile for those with power who know they are human beings like the rest of us. And none of us should take any of this too seriously.

★ Finding a way to reuse something you were originally going to throw away. Crafty repurposing smile.

★ Piñatas. This gets smiles because it means you're at a party, it means you get swing wildly at an object with a bat, it means there will eventually be candies or little novelties raining down from said beaten object, and it means you may get to see a scuffle on the ground for the previously mentioned goodies.

Christmas crackers. They just look festive, but then there's the snap and the little toy inside and the little piece of paper with the corny joke on it. And let's not forget the tissue paper crown. There's always one family member who wears it all through dinner. Jolly, wine-soaked smile.

★ Snow cones. This is leisure refreshment for warm days. Syrupy, icy smile.

★ A clean car. Floor mats vacuumed and free of dead leaves or sand, no paper straw wrappers under the seats, no stray pennies, no dust on the dash, and no smudges on the windows. There's a peaceful calm to a clean car.

★ Cat footprints on a car window. While it may, at first, be a little annoying, there's something sweet about tiny little tracks across the windshield.

Getting into a cab and it either doesn't stink or doesn't smell like cologne.

 Seeing someone wearing a purple lace face mask and full length cape at a Prince concert. That right there is a superfan, someone who owns more than one raspberry beret and knows exactly what it sounds like when doves cry.

★ Freshly painted walls. It's a nice, fresh start, and who doesn't love a fresh start. Extra smile if you got to pick the color. Another extra smile if it looks even better than you imagined.

★ Newly refinished floors. Another fresh start, this time giving new life to something that had seen its share of wear.

★ Seeing and hearing someone crack up over a joke. It's nice to witness someone laugh with total abandon, letting go of all other thoughts and just cackling at the humor of something said or read.

★ Men in leotards—always good for a smile and a chuckle.

★ Walk-a-thons. These are such a sincere way to raise money for a cause. Sure, it's donations based on estimations of how far someone is willing or able to walk in order to make some sort of change in the world. But giving kids a dollar for every lap they complete in order to buy new books for the library is noble and deserves a bunch of smiles.

★ Jack o' lanterns. Some people get super crafty, some keep it traditional. Extra smiles if you saved the seeds and toasted them.

★ Sea otters opening shells on their tummies. Beyond cute and a sure-fire smile generator.

★ Thinking about the best time you ever had with your closest friend. Try and single out the one time that was just the very best. It might be when you couldn't stop laughing, or maybe you can't believe you didn't get caught doing something you shouldn't have, or just the time your friend was there when you needed someone who understands you like no one else. Here's to closest friends and the smiles they generate.

The human capacity for kindness and love. This is limitless, as is the number of smiles that can come from thinking about this.

 Rain. It waters the plants, it cleans away the grime, it freshens the air, it makes for a good excuse to stay in instead of going to that party you know will be boring. Thanks, rain.

★ Old typewriters. They were once the pinnacle of technology and they were at the forefront of design, as well. Elegant or slick modern, they weren't just a piece of office equipment. The clack of the keys and the dinging bell of the return made crafting something written almost musical. Smile for these little printers.

★ Homemade musical instruments. People make ukuleles out of cigar boxes and kids try (usually in vain) to make flutes from bamboo shoots. They want to *make* music, from start to finish.

★ You aren't currently freefalling from an airplane without a parachute. What a relief, right?

★ Ren Faire people who forget that in Renaissance times, everyone smelled terrible and had some sort of disease. This blissful, intentional ignorance in the pursuit of a reimagined and fetishized revisionist history deserves a smile for effort.

★ Crazy hair colors. Extra smile if it's an old lady with bright magenta hair. Why the hell not?

★ Hospice workers. These people are angels, giving their all to the dying and those who feel like dying because of the loss of a loved one. They provide comfort and ease and plenty of smiles in times when all three are in short supply.

Clear umbrellas. Just because the sky is gray doesn't mean you don't want to see it.

People's random inventions. Some people are always trying to come up with new gadgets or new fixes to old problems. Sometimes these people are successful. Sometimes, well . . . they mean well. But they tried. Smile for good effort.

★ When you are walking toward someone and you each move in the same directions to get out of each other's way. Extra smile if one of you takes the cheesy route and asks, "Shall we dance?"

★ Hearing '80s alternative music at the grocery store. Perusing the soup aisle to the strains of Berlin's "Metro" is a smile-worthy occurrence, if for no other reason than the randomness of it all.

★ Angry notes written by seven-year-olds. When a kid takes out their frustration in writing, they let it all out. Granted, they haven't yet learned the finer points of filleting with words or even some of the more choice phrases to express total rage. As a result, the note comes across as charming instead of venomous.

★ Watching someone walk in platform boots. This is a literal balancing act. There may be a part of you waiting for the wearer to take a tumble, but the Clydesdale-style clomping itself is worth a smile.

★ The ridiculous things we do for fashion. Giant shoulder pads, super pointy-toed shoes, multiple petticoats, bright blue eye shadow, wide ties, acid wash denim, thin leather headbands. Shame smiles.

★ Fashion hindsight. We can look back at how ridiculous we were, feeling confident in our get-ups that are cool now but won't be so hot in ten years. Ah, well.

★ Seeing other people's doodles on notes. This little insight into someone's thought process, getting to see the other bits of information or concern that float through their head and onto the page is curious and deserves a smile.

★ Photobombing. Totally worth googling.

Yo-yo tricks. Corny, but still pretty amazing.

 Yo Yo Ma. Not corny, actually really funny and very amazing when it comes to the cello.

★ Novelty t-shirts on unlikely people. A lone grandpa wearing an "I'm With Stupid" shirt. A third world freedom fighter in news footage wearing an "I Hate Mondays" tee.

★ Old elementary school film strips. The lights would dim and out would come the projector on the metal cart. The teacher would feed the strip into the projector and onto the screen would come a grainy film about the periodic table of elements or America's founding fathers. Always a nice break during the class day and something that younger generations are missing out on.

Class photos. The haircuts, the names you'd forgotten, the one kid whose mom made him wear a bow tie to picture day. Nostalgia smile.

The jiggly, inflatable stick man at car dealerships. How this helps to gain customers and sell cars is unknown. But it is ridiculous and random and silly. Smile.

★ Old fancy handwriting. There was a time when much care was put into things written down. They used fancy pens, too. It may be a little difficult to read now, but those sweeping scrolls and delicate curls deserve appreciation and a smile.

★ Imagining Randy Newman writing and performing the theme song for the next James Bond film. Basically, it will sound like all the rest of his songs and make you wonder if Pixar is now involved in the Bond franchise.

★ Life as you know it right now. Close this book for a second and look around you. Wherever you are, I guarantee there is something, however insignificant, that will make you smile. Reasons to smile abound.